THE NEWS

KT-174-497

Bones EDITION

Ellen Marcus

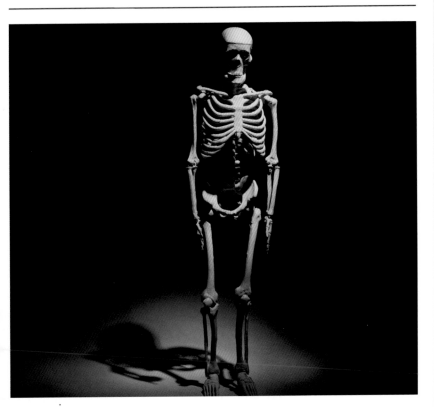

A word from our editor

SOME people think skeletons are creepy. But what would it be like if you didn't have one?

You'd just be a big blob of skin and hair and squashy intestines. Now that's creepy!

Do you think you'd be able to slide under doorways? Or squeeze into a padded bag and put yourself through the post?

It might sound like fun, but even those things would be impossible—if you didn't have a skeleton, you would not be able to move at all.

In this edition of *The News*, we're boning up on the human skeleton. You'll discover that there's a lot more to it than meets the eye.

Daily spot

The bumpy bone that sticks out just above your foot isn't your anklebone. It's the knob on the end of your shinbone.

The bare bones

What's holding you together?

Y OUR SKELETON is your body's frame. It's very strong. It's also perfectly balanced. It allows you to stand up straight and walk, run, skip, hop—even do somersaults (*say sum-er-salts*) if you want.

Of course, your skeleton wasn't always upright and balanced. Look at a toddler trying to walk. It's hard work.

The toddler's skeleton is not strong enough to support its weight. And some bits are too big or too small, so it can't balance very well.

Toddlers often topple over. That's because they're top-heavy. Their heads are too big and their feet are too little. As their skeleton takes shape, all that changes.

Thank goodness. If we kept falling over, we'd never get anything done.

You need your skeleton for protection. You could think of it as a special suit of armour that you wear on the inside.

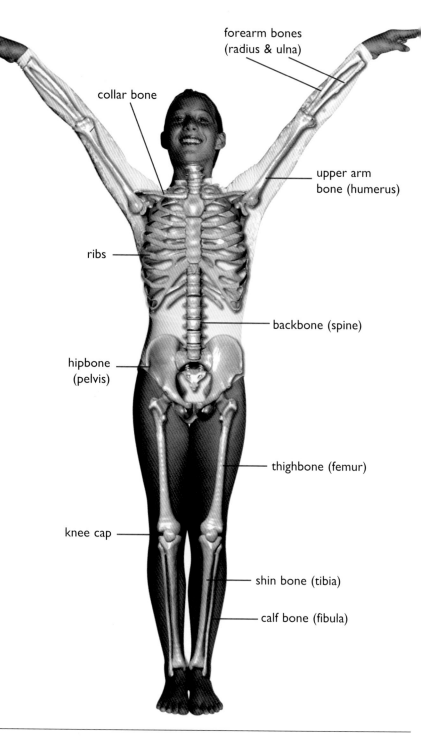

forearm bones
(radius & ulna)

collar bone

upper arm
bone (humerus)

ribs

backbone (spine)

hipbone
(pelvis)

thighbone (femur)

knee cap

shin bone (tibia)

calf bone (fibula)

Your skull is like a helmet. It protects your brain. It also protects the sensitive workings of your eyes and ears.

Your ribs and **sternum** (say *stir-num*) are just like a **breastplate** on a suit of armour. They protect your heart and lungs.

Your backbone is also part of your armour. It forms a bony tunnel. Your delicate spinal cord runs through the centre of the tunnel. Your backbone keeps your spinal cord safe from harm.

And your **pelvis** (say *pell-viss*) is like a sturdy pair of underpants! It shelters your bladder and intestines.

The heel bone's connected to the leg bone. The leg bone's connected to the hipbone. The hipbone's connected to the backbone. The backbone's connected to the...

Your pelvic bones are like a pair of tough undies!

Your skull is your brain's helmet.

Did you know?

Bones start out as a tough, rubbery substance called **cartilage** (say *car-till-idge*). Minerals in the body make the cartilage harder and stronger. Before long, it turns into bone.

Bone matter

What's the weight?

HAVE YOU ever seen an aluminium baseball bat? Well, your bones are a bit like that. They are strong but not heavy or hard to move. Bones are tough but light.

Of course, bones aren't hollow like a baseball bat.

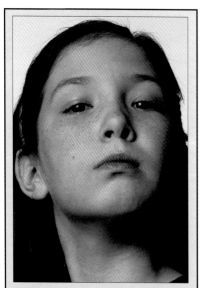

Did you know?

The pointy end of your nose is soft and rubbery. That's because it is made out of cartilage, not bone.

Hope the ball hits his bat and not his femur!

As well as being strong and light, your bones are alive! And they are very busy.

Bones make most of your body's blood cells. They also store special minerals that your body needs to stay healthy.

One of these minerals is **calcium** (say *kal-see-um*). Calcium is a very important mineral because it keeps your bones and teeth strong.

Your thighbone is called a femur (say *fee-ma*). It is one of the busiest bones in your body. Your femur has three main parts that work to keep your body strong and healthy.

So, that dry old bone your dog drags around the back-yard is nothing like your own healthy, living bones.

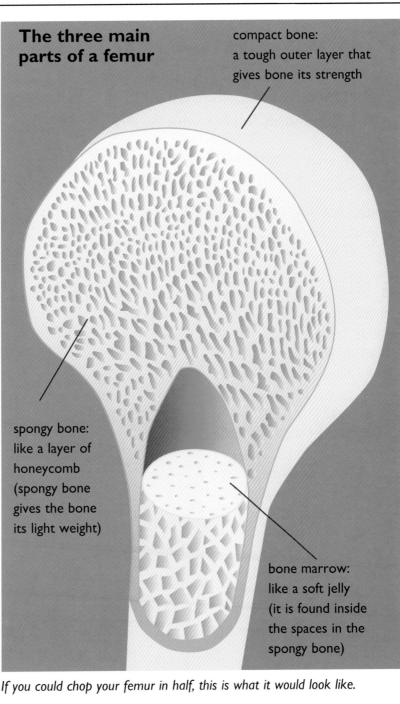

The three main parts of a femur

compact bone:
a tough outer layer that gives bone its strength

spongy bone:
like a layer of honeycomb
(spongy bone gives the bone its light weight)

bone marrow:
like a soft jelly
(it is found inside the spaces in the spongy bone)

If you could chop your femur in half, this is what it would look like.

He looks sad. Perhaps he has forgotten where he buried his bone!

Fact of the day

Your femur is the biggest, strongest, heaviest bone in your body. It has your body's largest supply of bone marrow.

Word of the day

BONE MARROW—a soft jelly inside most bones. It makes red blood cells that keep you healthy.

Sticks and stones

Will break my bones…but what about the monkey bars?
An interview with Sophie who found out the hard way!

Sophie, tell me about the day you broke your arm.
I was on the school monkey bars. I was doing threes. I was half way across and I stopped to talk to my friend. As I was hanging there talking, the girl behind me crashed into me. I fell and landed on my arm.

Did it hurt?
It really hurt! I was dizzy and crying. Everyone crowded around. My friends carried me to the duty teacher. She took me to sick bay and Dad took me to the doctor.

What did the doctor do?
The doctor felt my wrist. Then she said, "You better go to X-ray." The nurse put my arm in a sling.

What happened at the X-ray place?
Dad had to sit behind a wall to protect him from the rays. I put on a special apron made of lead. It protected my body so that only my arm got zapped.

They kept turning my arm to get the right position. It hurt heaps. Then, we took the X-rays back to the doctor.

What did the doctor say this time?

She looked at the X-ray, and she said, "You've got a broken wrist." Then she put a plaster cast on. It went up to my elbow. She said I couldn't get it signed for a couple of days because it had to set.

Was the plaster annoying?

Not really. I did have to put a plastic bag over it to have a shower. The plaster would be wrecked if it got wet.

My arm kept on hurting, especially at night. I had to sleep on the floor because I couldn't climb up into my bunk.

When did you have the cast removed?

After four weeks. The doctor cut it off with giant scissors. It didn't hurt, but it really stank because I hadn't washed my arm for a month!

How was your arm?

Perfect. But I had to wait another two weeks before I could play on the monkey bars again.

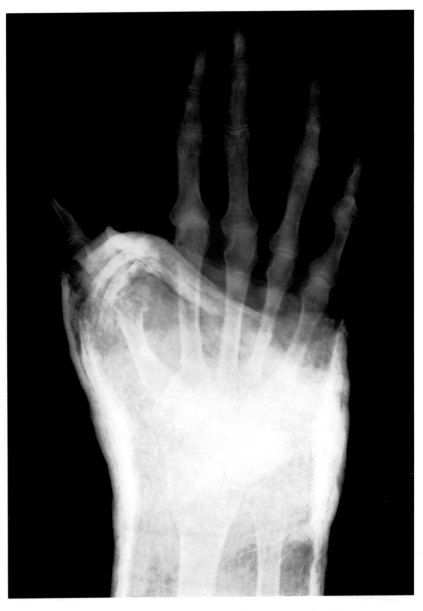

X-ray of a hand in a plaster cast. The big white area is the plaster.

Did you know?

The ribs are like a cage with movable bars. The muscles between the ribs lift the cage upwards and outward. This gives the lungs room to fill with air so you can breathe.

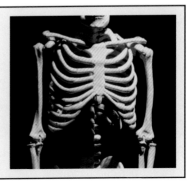

Give me a break?

No, thank you!

MEDICAL PEOPLE have special names for breaks in bones. A break is called a fracture. There are different types of fractures. Some are a lot more serious than others.

A compound fracture is serious because the broken bone sticks out through the skin. Ouch! If it is not treated properly, germs can get in through the break in the skin and infect the bone.

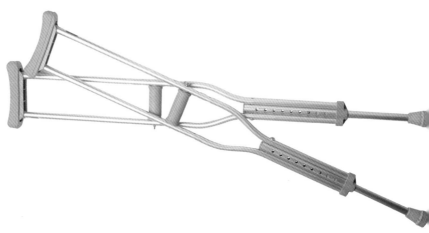

Crutches can give a broken leg time to heal. The patient can walk about, without putting any pressure on the broken bone.

These green sticks are too bendy to snap in half easily—just like young bones! When the tree gets older, the sticks grow harder and bend less, so they snap more easily—like older bones.

A greenstick fracture is the least serious type of fracture. They are common in children because children's bones are soft and **flexible**, like green sticks—the little ends of branches on trees. The bone bends and breaks, but the break doesn't go all the way through the bone.

Fact of the day

Bone is always renewing itself. Old bone cells die and new bone cells replace them. That's why broken bones can heal. As long as the broken ends are held together, they will knit and the break will mend.

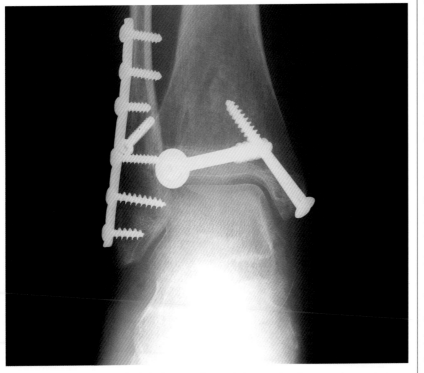

Sometimes, when you break bones, they might not heal properly on their own. Screws are used to keep the bones in the right place while they heal. You can see the screws in this X-ray.

Did you know?

Barry Sheene was a famous motorcyclist. He had a high-speed crash and broke both his legs. His bones were shattered. Doctors used 26 screws and plates to put the bones back together. After he was patched up, Barry was back racing his motorcycle again.

Lights please

IN 1895, a German scientist called Wilhelm Roentgen discovered a strange kind of light. It could shine through solid objects such as tin and books. It could even shine through skin. The light was so mysterious that he decided to call it "X-ray".

For two months, Roentgen worked his fingers to the bone experimenting with X-ray. He finally came up with a way of taking photographs using his new X-ray light.

X-ray light was so useful, it wasn't long before doctors everywhere were using X-rays to see broken bones and other problems hidden deep inside their patients.

Fact of the day

The first full-length X-ray of a man showed more than just his skeleton. It even showed the keys in his pocket.

Hands down

Thumbs up.

H ERE'S A challenge. See how long you can go without using your thumbs.

Start from the time you get up in the morning. Brushing your teeth won't be too hard. But how will you turn on the taps? And I hope you don't have too many buttons on your clothes…

The human hand is a remarkable tool, especially because of the thumb.

The bones of the thumb go right down into the palm of the hand. The thumb is long and very mobile. It can touch the tips of each finger. This movement helps us do many things. It is called the "pincer grip".

Chimpanzees have big toes that work a lot like our thumbs. This means they can grab things with their feet.

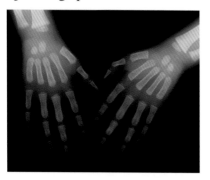

X-ray of a child's hands. You can see the bones, but not the cartilage.

Bone sp●t

Dinosaurs take the prize for having the longest arm bones. Some had arms up to 3 metres (9 ft) long!

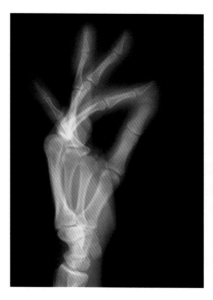

Did you know?

Cartilage does not show up on X-rays. Since babies' bones are mostly cartilage, their skeletons look quite strange if X-rayed.

The pincer grip is good for getting peanuts out of a packet!

Keep moving!

Exercise makes bones better.

Keep your bones healthy through sport or play.

EXERCISE IS good for your bones. When you move, your muscles pull on your bones. This sends a message to your bones that it's time for action. Action makes your bones grow stronger and renew themselves.

The best exercises for bones are "weight-bearing" exercises.

This is when you move the weight of your body without help from other equipment. Walking, running and dancing are weight-bearing exercises.

As people get older, their bones stop renewing as fast as they used to. If not cared for, old bones can become **brittle**. Brittle bones break easily and take a long time to mend.

Fact of the day

Osteoporosis (say os-te-o-por-row-sis) is a bone disease that makes bones break easily. It happens when bones don't have enough calcium.

Bone appétit!

Good eating for healthy bones.

STRONG HEALTHY bones need a good supply of the mineral called calcium. Calcium makes bones hard and gives them strength.

Our bodies cannot produce calcium, so we have to get it from food. Not all food has calcium in it, and different food has different amounts of calcium. Children need three serves of calcium a day to keep their bones healthy.

How much food is three serves of calcium? Well, unless you have an enormous appetite, it is easier to get all the calcium you need from dairy products.

You could eat 60 slices of wholemeal bread… or 18 oranges…or 3kg (6$\frac{1}{2}$ lbs) of broccoli… or…if you like your calcium on the run, you can have a couple of cheese slices, a few spoonfuls of yoghurt and a glass of milk.

Fact of the day

Blackboard chalk is made of calcium. But it's not the same calcium that's in your bones. The calcium in chalk comes from the shells of tiny dead sea creatures.

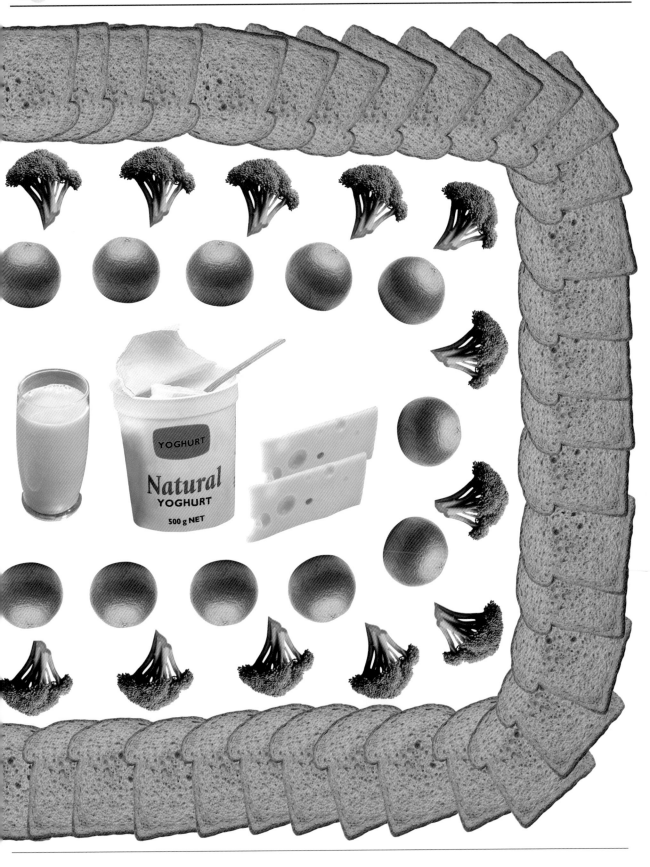

Baby bones

Imagine… if a baby could speak before it was born.

I'M GETTING born tomorrow. I can't wait. It's really cramped in here. And I want to meet my family. I can hear them out there. They make heaps of noise. They sound like fun.

I was really worried about getting born. I thought I might get squashed. But yesterday I heard the midwife tell Mum all about it.

The midwife said that babies' bones are really soft. She said our bones bend easily and can squash up. This makes it easier for us to squeeze out into the world

Phew! That's a relief.

But there's one thing the midwife said that I'm not happy about. She said I might have a pointy head! This is because the bones in my skull have not joined up yet. Yuk.

But she told Mum not to worry—it's not forever. Soon after I get born, the bones in my skull will join up. Then my head will be perfect.

So, I've decided to stop worrying. It's giving me a headache.

Get a head!

Make a skull mask.

Have you ever wondered what your own skull looks like? You can make a model using papier-mache.

This model skull will also have a moveable jaw with a hinge joint. Say aahh!

You will need:

- a balloon
- plain paper, torn into pieces
- craft glue
- paintbrushes and paint
- a strip of cardboard to make the jaw (cereal box cardboard will do)
- 2 paper fasteners for the hinge joint.

What to do:

1 Blow up the balloon until it's the size of your head.
2 Brush glue over half of the balloon and paste the paper pieces onto it. Leave spaces for your eyes.
3 Paint another layer of glue over the paper.
4 Repeat steps 2–4 several times.
5 When the glue is dry, burst the balloon.
6 Paint shadows around each eye and a shadow for your nose.
7 Use the paper fasteners to join the cardboard strip to the bottom of the skull.
8 Paint on teeth or make them out of cardboard and glue them on!

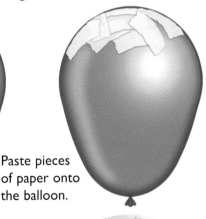

Blow up the balloon to the size of your head.

Paste pieces of paper onto the balloon.

Leave holes for eyes. When the glue is dry, burst the balloon.

Paint and join the cardboard jaw to the mask using paper fasteners.

Did you know?

Many birds have holes in their skulls. This makes the bird lighter and therefore helps it to fly.

Animal antics

We can learn a lot about animals from their bones.

A goat has no top front teeth. It uses its tongue and lips to pull grass. Goats have special joints in their jaws. This means they can slide their jaws front-to-back and side-to-side. All the better for **grinding** grass.

Dogs have big noses for smelling. They have at least 100 million "smelling cells". Humans only have about 5 million.

inside a flipper

Inside the flippers of porpoises, dolphins, whales, tortoises and sea lions, are bones that look just like arm bones. They even have finger bones!

Call the dentist

Please!

This is a coyote (say ky-oh-tea) skull. A coyote is a wild dog. Notice the long nose bone.

Gibbons have very long arms so they can swing through the treetops. Their extra-long forearms mean they have a very wide swing. This gives them extra speed.

I N 1898, two lions in Kenya attacked and ate more than 130 railway workers.

Some **zoologists** (say *zoo-ol-a-jists*) examined the skulls of the lions. They found that the lions had terrible teeth and jaws. The zoologists worked out that this is why the lions attacked the people.

Both lions had broken or wobbly teeth, and painful abscesses. One of them even had a broken jaw. They were in need of a good dentist.

The zoologists think that the lions attacked because people are much easier to catch and kill (and chew on) than normal **prey**.

Bones that creak in the night

Spooky skeletons.

WHY DO some people think skeletons are creepy? It might be because, for centuries, the skeleton has been a symbol of death. Here are just some of the ghostly forms it takes.

The skull and crossbones are often used as a warning. If it appears on the label of a bottle or container, be very careful. Whatever is inside is dangerous. Never swallow, smell or touch anything with a skull and crossbones label.

The skull and crossbones flag of pirate ships was called the Jolly Roger. It was designed to scare the pirates' victims. But some pirates changed the design to suit themselves.

A famous pirate called Bartholomew Roberts had his own flag designed. It showed him standing on the skulls of his two greatest enemies.

An example of a Jolly Roger design. Not the most welcoming flag!

The Grim Reaper has been a symbol of death for centuries.

POISON

No one would drink from a bottle with a label like this.

Funny bones

To really crack you up.

Dem bones rap

Good strong bones will keep you goin'
Till you're twenty, they'll keep growin'
Feed them, walk them, and protect them
Bones are great,
So don't neglect them.

a poem by Izzy Jointed

Editorial

Letters
to the editor

EVERYONE says the human skeleton is great because we walk upright on two legs. But is it really the best way to go?

Walking on two legs has slowed humans down quite a bit. It also means that we are not as strong or agile as some of our four-legged friends.

We can't climb trees as well as monkeys. We can't carry people around like camels and horses can, and we can't run as fast as cheetahs.

On the other hand, because we only use two legs to walk, we have two spare limbs. That means we can get lots of things done! Because we have arms and hands, we can build amazing things.

We can build cars and they give us speed. We can build aeroplanes that allow us to fly. We can even build ladders and cranes and space shuttles. So, we can do everything animals can, and more.

Walking upright may be a good move after all.

Dear Editor,
I wish my owner would buy a hat for winter. Doesn't she know that 70% of her body's heat is lost through her head? She's got really short hair and I'm the coldest skull around.

From CHILLY TOP

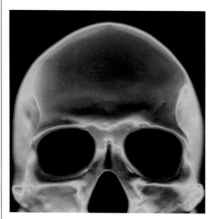

The editor.

Dear Editor,
A cold skull is nothing. My owner plays rugby and I'm scared stiff. What if I get a serious injury? Necks weren't made for such dangerous sports.

From SCARED STIFF NECK

Dear Editor,
I agree with Scared Stiff Neck. Kids need to care for their spines. My owner slumps all over the place and then whinges about backache. Don't these kids know how important good posture is?

From SIT UP STRAIGHT

Luckily for his skull, he is wearing a good helmet.

Paging Dr Elle Bow

Dear Dr Elle,
I'm in a panic. I'm allergic to dairy products. How will I ever get enough calcium to keep my bones healthy?

From BILLY BONES

DR ELLE: Chill out! There are plenty of other ways of getting calcium. Eating fish (especially tuna) is good. Soy products, like **tofu** *and soy milk, have calcium. So do Chinese vegetables and tahini, which is a spread made from sesame seeds. You'll be fine. I can feel it in my bones.*

Dear Dr Elle,
My sister says she is double-jointed and that's why she can do the splits. Is that true?

From ANNA FONTEYN

DR ELLE: Your sister has been listening to silly myths. There is no such thing as a double joint. Some people are more flexible than others, that's all. Who cares if you can't do the splits? Why don't you learn to sing? It's much more entertaining.

Canned sardines are a good source of calcium.

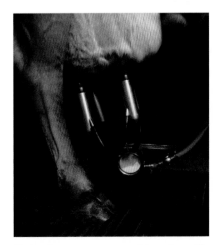

Dairy farmers use machines to milk their cows.

There is no such thing as a double joint. It takes years of practice to make your body do this.

Further resources

BOOKS

There are stacks of great books about the human body and the skeleton. Some are more involved than others.

When it comes to learning about the human body, it's best to learn the basics first. Later on, you can explore the details. Some great books are listed below.

Carol Ballard *The Human Body: The Skeleton and Muscular System* Hove Publishers

Katherine Goode *The Skeleton and Muscles* Macmillan Education

Steve Parker *Skeleton* Franklin Watts

The Reader's Digest Children's Book of the Human Body

Anna Sandeman *Your Body: Bones* Watts

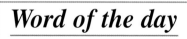

Word of the day

MANDIBLE—(say *man-da-bl*) the jawbone.

INTERNET

There are some terrific facts about bones and fractures on the Kids Health site at: www.kidshealth.org/kid/ Follow the links to My Body or search the site for "bones".

Take a bones tour with Flint, the frill-necked lizard: www.arthritiswa.org.au/dem bones/sport.shtml

Find out more about your skeleton with Mr Bones at: www.bayfront.org/explore/ke 0.html

Look up skeleton or bones on a search engine or on-line encyclopaedia.

PLACES

Museums are a great place to see skeletons—check out the human and animal sections. Your local medical clinic should have pamphlets about how to care for your bones.

JOKES

Q. What did the **palaeontologist** (say *pay-lee-on-toll-oh-jist*) yell when she dug up a pelvic bone?

A. *Hip, hip, hooray!*

Q. Who are the best people to run a haunted house?

A. *A skeleton staff.*

Q. How did the skeleton escape from the laboratory?

A. *He used his skeleton key.*

Q. What did the thighbone say to the hipbone?

A. *Nice joint, think I'll hang around.*

Chew on this

Did you know that you have 22 bones in your skull? But you can only move one of them. Can you guess which one? If you guess aloud, this bone will move. That's right! It's your jawbone.

Glossary

BREASTPLATE—armour for across the chest.

BRITTLE—likely to break easily.

CALCIUM—(say *kal-see-um*) a soft silver-white metal that is found in limestone and chalk, and in teeth and bones.

CARTILAGE—(say *car-till-idge*) a firm, elastic substance forming part of your bone structure.

FLEXIBLE—easily bent or stretched.

GRINDING—crushing into fine bits.

PALAEONTOLOGIST—(say *pay-lee-on-toll-oh-jist*) a scientist who studies the fossils of plants and animals.

PELVIS—(say *pell-viss*) the ring of bone made up of the lower part of your backbone and your two hips, and the empty space it forms.

PREY—an animal hunted for food by another.

STERNUM—(say *stir-num*) the breastbone.

TOFU—a white jelly-like substance made from soybean milk.

ZOOLOGISTS—(say *zoo-ol-a-jists*) scientists who study animal life.

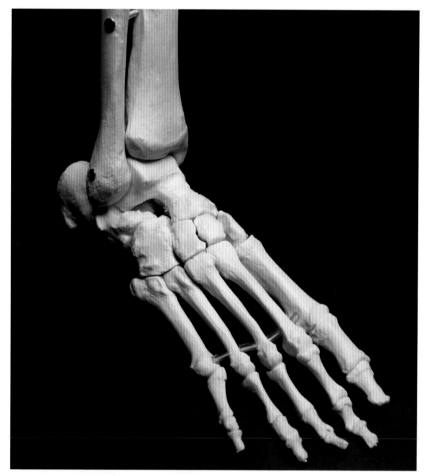

There are 206 bones in the adult human skeleton—106 of these bones are found in the hands and feet.

Did you know?

The euoplocephalus (say *you-op-low-kef-a-lus*) was a very bony type of dinosaur. It had a club on the end of its tail made of bone. And it even had an extra set of eyelids that were made of bone!

Bone n●tes

The first flutes were made from the hollow leg bones of sheep. Holes were punched along the bone so that the person playing the flute could play a range of musical notes.

Index

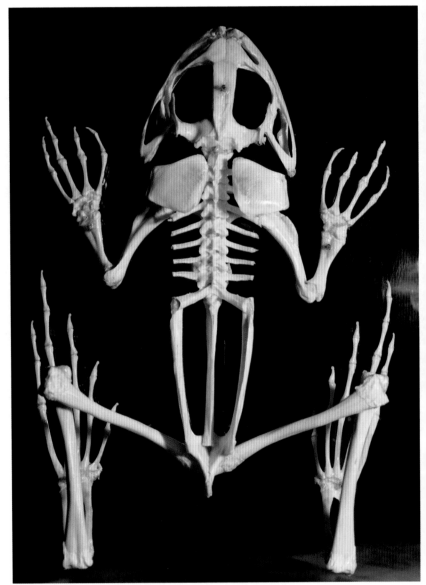

When you look at a bullfrog skeleton, you can see that it has very long bones in its back legs. These long bones help bullfrogs to jump high and leap a long way.